Does God Exist?

Does God Exist?

The Question Answered

James Slater

The Pentland Press Limited
Edinburgh • Cambridge • Durham • USA

© James Slater 1995

First published in 1995 by
The Pentland Press Ltd.
1 Hutton Close
South Church
Bishop Auckland
Durham

British Library Cataloguing in Publication Data.
A Catalogue record for this book is available
from the British Library.

ISBN 1 85821 331 2

Typeset by CBS, Felixstowe, Suffolk
Printed and bound by Antony Rowe Ltd., Chippenham

INDEX

DOES GOD EXIST?

DOES GOD EXIST? If you were asked that question how would you answer? Would you be able to prove beyond all doubt that there is an unseen Higher Power in control of all?

This question has been asked down through the centuries, and I believe it is asked more often now than ever before. I believe too that the one who asks such a question does so not because of any doubts he or she may have, but because they know full well that there is a Supreme Being to whom they are accountable, and they would prefer it were not so. Indeed, the evidence of the existence of God is so manifest that the questioner will have a more difficult task in proving the case that there is no God than I will have in proving otherwise.

It is not necessary to defend God; He is omnipotent. My purpose in writing these notes is to give help to any believer who may not be able to gainsay the arguments of the atheist. There are many young believers in our colleges and universities who have to make a stand against the atheism of some of their teachers and lecturers. For in academic and religious circles, the main aim of some seems to be to disprove all that is of

1

God and His Word.

Most will agree that all materials require a First Cause to explain how and when all was brought into being. Is there a Creator God? Or did all come into being by a process of evolution?

Someone may pose this question: if all things require a First Cause, how do you justify the claim for an eternal God, without beginning, and without end? This, we must admit, is beyond our finite comprehension. Here we hold humbly to a simple faith in an Almighty and Omniscient God, something we have proved in life and experience, but which defies definition. The Atheist has said: we cannot see God. How then can His existence be proved? We affirm that things *can* be proved that cannot be seen. What about the element we call 'air'? we cannot see it, but we can prove it is around us. We feel it in our face, there is the ripple on the water, and its power in the raging storm and it is an essential for sustaining life.

The analogy is obvious. God is omnipresent, we cannot see Him, but His power is evident to all but the willingly ignorant. He is the One of Whom it is written, 'In whose hand is the soul of every living thing, and the breath of all mankind.' (Job 12:10.)

In the following pages we present the evidence. There is the voice of creation: 'For the invisible things of Him from the creation of the world are clearly seen, being understood by the things that are made, even His eternal power and Godhead; so that they are without excuse.' (Romans 1:20).

The nation of Israel, in its remarkable history and survival, is a very present witness to the existence of God.

What of the Bible? That remarkable book, the life-giving Word of God! Millions of men and women have proved its worth and power. It has been banned and burned, many have suffered martyrdom for it, and despite all efforts to have it suppressed, we still have it in our hands today.

Man, the masterpiece of creation, is shown to be the only creature to have inherent spiritual desires and aspirations, this through his being created in the 'image of God' (Genesis 1:26).

The writer, now ninety years of age, tells of his own experience of redeeming grace in seventy years of living links with the Lord Jesus, owning Him Christ and Lord and seeking to live and serve according to the precepts of the Holy Scriptures.

The question is often asked, 'If there is a God of love up there, why have we the disasters, plagues, and famines that beset our planet today?' This we have endeavoured to answer.

Whether all these questions have been fairly and successfully answered or not, the reader will judge. We trust that some will benefit from what has been presented, and find assurance in that 'the Most High ruleth in the kingdom of men.' *All* is under divine control: He is there – Omniscient, Omnipresent, and Omnipotent, the eternal God, 'upholding all things by the word of His power' (Hebrew 1:3).

THE VOICE OF CREATION

'The heavens declare the glory of God, and the firmament sheweth His handiwork. Day unto day uttereth speech, and night unto night sheweth knowledge. There is no speech nor language; their voice is not heard. Their line is gone out through all the earth, and their words to the end of the world' (Psalm 19:1-4).

I would challenge any man or woman, out on a clear and frosty night and away from the city lights, to look up to the star-filled dome of the heavens and say with honest conviction, 'There is no God.'

How did these millions of stars come into being? How did each find its particular orbit? What power keeps them in place and how are they controlled?

The patriarch Job, over three thousand years ago, made this terse statement: 'He hangeth the earth upon nothing' (Job 26:7). Astronomers, past and present, have proved to us the truth of this, and with all the modern equipment for communication and measurement, they have not yet found a limit to the vastness of space. Distance there is measured in light years (the distance which light travels in a year at a speed of 186,000 miles per second), and the figures used in calculations are millions and thousands of millions.

Each star and planet has its orbit and revolving routine; the earth performs its daily rotation of twenty-four hours on its axis and its yearly orbit of some 600 million miles around the blazing sun. How was it kindled?

Every living thing depends on the sun. The distance the earth is from the sun is correct for the maintenance of life here, as are the component parts of the various elements in the air, in the sea, and in the soil. All is arranged and measured in perfection so that as the seasons continue in the ordered cycle (See Genesis 8:22), the earth yields the sustenance needful for every living animal and plant.

The timing of the cycles of the sun, the stars and the planets is such that lunar and solar eclipses can be accurately foretold years in advance. So too is the annual record and timing of tides prepared for seamen, all based on the unerring cycle of the sun and the moon.

Very many learned scientists, such as Charles Darwin and men of like mind, tell us that all those wonders of the universe emerged in a process of evolution. According to them, all life came originally from the sea and over millions of years the operation of natural selection (the survival of the fittest) has brought us life in all the varied forms in which we have it today. We pose the question: where did this sea come from in the first instance? and if man is descended from the ape, why are there still apes in the jungles of the world? Will they yet become human?

Another theory of the origin of the universe is that the stars and planets were formed as the result of a massive explosion, 'The Big Bang'. This, some scientists affirm, took place millions of years ago. The fragments from it were scattered in all directions and became what we now see as the starry dome of the heavens. Again the question arises, where and how did the material for the Big Bang originate?

Wiser men and women turn away from the folly of such theories, and simply and trustfully accept the teaching of the Holy Scriptures. 'By faith we understand that the worlds were framed by the word of God, so that the things that are seen were not made of the things which do appear' (Hebrews 11:3). 'By the word of the Lord were the heavens made; and all the host of them by the breath of His mouth. He gathereth the waters of the sea together as a heap:' (the earth is a globe, so that contrary to appearances, the surface of the oceans is curved and not flat as it appears to be). 'For He spake and it was done, He commanded and it stood fast' (Psalm 33:6-9).

Well might we marvel and wonder as we ponder the vastness of unmeasured space and what is there displayed. There is the massive Betelgeuse in the constellation of Orion, some 500 million miles in circumference, and our own planet Earth, a mere 25,000 miles round at the equator. The planet Neptune takes 176 years in its orbit of the sun, while Pluto (the most distant of the planets in our solar system) has an orbit of some 240 years. It is indeed a humbling point to contemplate. Well might we echo the words of the Psalmist, 'When I consider the heavens, the work of Thy fingers, the moon and the stars which

Thou hast ordained; what is man that Thou art mindful of him? And the son of man that Thou visitest him?' (Psalm 8:4).

At this moment here on earth marvels and wonders are to be found all around us. We have only to recall the migratory cycle of the salmon, the homing instinct of the pigeon, or the diverse patterns of migration of other species of bird. The eels from our rivers find their way across the Atlantic Ocean to the depths of the Sargasso Sea, there to breed and grow. The young of all birds and animals develop the same characteristic markings as their forebears and follow their habits of nesting or hunting. All bear witness to the amazing design of an all-wise God.

ISRAEL - A CHOSEN NATION

The fact that there is a nation called Israel in Palestine today bears living witness to the existence of God. Its origin, its history and its survival are truly remarkable. It began with the call by the God of Abraham while he dwelt in the land of Haran. 'Now the Lord said to Abraham, "Get thee out of thy country, and from thy kindred, and from thy father's house, unto a land which I will shew thee, and I will make of thee a great nation."' (Genesis 12:1-2). 'And He gave him the covenant of circumcision and so Abraham begat Isaac, . . . and Isaac begat Jacob; and Jacob begat the twelve patriarchs' (Acts 7:8).

The sons of Jacob, (later called Israel), because of famine went down to Egypt; they continued in that land for some 400 years, and there multiplied and grew. Moses was born and grew up there, and it was under his leadership that they were brought out from the bondage they endured while in Egypt. After forty years of wandering they came into the promised land of Canaan, to live there under prophets, judges, and kings. The last king of Judah was Zedekiah. He was carried off captive into Babylon (The glory of that Babylon has perished; Israel still survives), where he died in prison during the captivity which was to last for seventy years. This bondage was the judgment of God because of the rebellion and idolatry of the Israelites. Their rather chequered history, as recorded in the Old Testament, was ever marked by periods of rebellion and repentance.

In the epoch of the New Testament the Jews were under the rule of Rome. Their Messiah came and was rejected; 'He came unto His own, and His own people received Him not' (John 1:11). He was in their midst for thirty-three years, proving to them who He was and why He came. Before He ascended, He foretold the judgment that was to come upon the nation and the destruction of the temple. This was fulfilled in A.D. 70, when Titus laid Jerusalem waste and the temple was destroyed by fire. (See Matthew 24:1).

Over the centuries the Jews have been dispersed among the nations; there is scarcely a nation where there are not resident Jews. Wherever the Jews have lived they have kept their own identity and customs, and always lived with their heart towards Jerusalem, their promised home. Even their physical features, dress and characteristics have been more or less preserved. It is marvellous how they have survived, a nation without a king for two thousand years, downtrodden and despised in almost every land where they have settled.

Any who are interested in the history of Israel should read Deuteronomy chapters 28-30. Verse 1 of chapter 28 reads: 'And it shall come to pass, if thou shalt hearken diligently unto the voice of the Lord thy God, to observe and to do all His commandments which I command thee this day, that the Lord thy God will set thee high above all the nations of the earth.'

Throughout these chapters a detailed description is given of what would befall the people of Israel if they were disobedient, as well as the blessings that would be theirs if they sought after God and obeyed His commands. How truly has all come to pass!

The question may be asked, 'if Israel is a people chosen of God, as they surely are, why have they been persecuted and despised as no other people have ever been?' I believe the main reason for the oppression and affliction they have had to endure is the rejection of their Messiah. While Pilate could find no fault in Him and sought to release Him, they clamoured for His death. They cried, 'His blood be on us and our children!' (Matthew 27:25). What a fearful harvest they have reaped!

In spite of all, their heart has ever been towards Jerusalem, and especially to the site where the temple stood. Britain was in the forefront of the efforts to settle them again as a nation in Palestine. The Balfour Declaration, issued by a British statesman Arthur J. Balfour in 1922, represented a major advance in the project. On May 21st 1948 the flag of Israel was hoisted in Palestine. After forty years they are still there, surrounded by hostile nations and in conflict with the displaced people in their midst. They are there, holding tenaciously to the traditions of their forebears and to the biblical promise of the land as their right under the covenant God made with Abraham. While we cannot condone their present activities directed against the resident Palestinians there, we cannot deny that the Divine promise will yet be fulfilled despite all that men or nations seek to do for or against that chosen nation.

An irony of this situation is that Arab and Jew both claim Abraham as their forefather; the Arab in virtue of his descent through Ishmael, and the Jew from Isaac.

The present area occupied by Israel is very limited, even though she expanded it in the Six-Day War so as to include the West Bank and the Gaza Strip. The territory God promised to Abraham extended from the Great River, the Euphrates, to the River of Egypt, the Nile. (See Genesis 15:18). This has been fully occupied on two occasions: under Joshua who led them into it from their wilderness journeys; and under Solomon the king (See Joshua 21:43 and 2 Chronicles 9:26). It is still destined to be the full extent of their possession.

THE BIBLE

'God who at sundry times and in diverse manners spake in time past unto the fathers by the prophets, hath in these last days spoken unto us by His Son, whom He hath appointed heir of all things, by whom also He made the worlds.' (Hebrews 1:1-2.)

So it has pleased the Almighty God to communicate with mortal man at different times and in diverse ways. How He did this is recorded for us in the Old and New Testament writings. When we turn to the New Testament, we have the writings of men who journeyed with our Lord Jesus, who 'were eye-witnesses of His majesty'. (2 Peter 1:16).

It is said of the record of Old Testament history and events, 'For whatsoever things were written aforetime were written for our learning, that we through patience and comfort of the Scriptures might have hope.' (Romans 15:4). The main purpose of the New Testament writings is stated by the apostle John: 'Many other signs truly did Jesus in the presence of His disciples, which are not written in this book: but these are written, that ye might believe that Jesus is the Christ, the Son of God, and that believing ye might have life through His Name.' (John 20:

30-31).

'All scripture is given by inspiration of God, and is profitable for doctrine, for reproof, for correction, for instruction in righteousness; that the man of God may be perfect, thoroughly furnished unto all good works.' (2 Timothy 3:16-17). 'For no prophecy ever came by the will of man; but holy men spake from God, being moved by the Holy Spirit.' (2 Peter 1:20-21).

Here we have the claim made by Peter and Paul that the Bible is the inspired word of God. The sceptic makes much of the fact that it was written by men. It is also true that we do not have the Holy Scriptures in their original form, as they were given to those who wrote them. Some material has been lost in copying errors and in translation, but the veracity and truth of the fundamental doctrines of Holy Writ, as given originally by God, stand firm and true.

'In the beginning God created the heavens and the earth' (Genesis 1:1). That is how we are introduced to the written revelation of God and His works. The second verse tells us of the movement of the Holy Spirit in a scene of chaos. It reads: 'And the earth was waste and void: and darkness was upon the face of the deep: and the Spirit of God moved upon the face of the waters.'

Time and again the Scriptures remind us that all was pronounced good that God created and made.

In Isaiah we read, 'For thus saith the Lord that created the heavens; God Himself that formed the earth and made it; He created it not a waste, He formed it to be inhabited.' (Isaiah 45:18).

It is evident from this that a calamity of some magnitude occurred between the first and second verses of Genesis, chapter 1.

Thomas Newberry, an eminent Bible scholar, points out very clearly in his booklet, *The Perfections and Excellencies of Holy Scripture*, that there is a period of time between these verses which we cannot measure, nor is its extent revealed to us. Doubtless it is millions of years.

Could this be a calamity that occurred when Satan and his angels rebelled? 'How art thou fallen from heaven, O Lucifer, son of the morning? For thou hast said in thine heart, I will ascend into heaven, I will exalt my throne above the stars of God, . . . I will be like the Most High.' (Isaiah 14:12-14).

There is sufficient time between the events recorded in the first two verses of Genesis, chapter 1 for the formation of all fossils and minerals, enough to satisfy any scientist who may be interested in this line of inquiry.

From the point when God said, 'Let there be light' (Genesis 1:3), He began a work of creation and reconstruction. The world of chaos was transformed and reformed, and *life* in all its variety, as we know it today, was created. From the dated genealogies in Holy Scripture we learn accurately that man was created around 4004 B.C. and has been on the earth now for some 6000 years.

Does this collection of writings, the Bible, prove the existence of God? Can we believe what we have just recorded concerning it? Is it truly a revelation from God, and can this be proved? We will endeavour to answer these questions by searching the Book.

Noah and his family were in the ark for a year and ten days while the flood was upon the earth. In Genesis 8:4 we read: 'And the ark rested in the seventh month, on the seventeenth day of the month, upon the mountains of Ararat.' Why mention that date? The answer is most interesting. It was on that day, some 2000 years later, that the Lord Jesus rose from the dead. The Passover was celebrated on the fourteenth day of the month, 'Christ our Passover is sacrificed for us,' (1 Corinthians 5:7). He died on that day and left the tomb three days later, on the seventeenth day. Is there a divine Hand in this, or was it coincidence?

Noah had three sons who, with their wives, were with him in the ark: they were Shem, Ham, and Japheth. The Bible tells us that, 'of these was the whole earth overspread.' The most casual of study will show that Shem is the father of the Semitic races, from Ham is descended the negroid ones, while Japheth is the forebear of other non-Semitic peoples. It is of interest to note that when we turn to the Acts of the Apostles, we find a representative man from each of these brought into the kingdom of God. In chapter 8:27 we read of the Ethiopian eunuch, the black man. In 9:1, we have Saul of Tarsus; while in 10:1 we are introduced to Cornelius, the non-Semitic Gentile.

'When Jesus was born in Bethlehem of Judea in the days of Herod the king, behold wise men came from the east to Jerusalem, saying, "Where is He that is born King of the Jews?" . . . And when Herod the king heard it he was troubled, and all Jerusalem with him, and gathering together all the chief priests and scribes, he inquired of them where Christ should be born.

and they said unto him, "In Bethlehem of Judea: for thus it is written by the prophet.'" (Matthew 2:1-5). A prophet called Micah made that prophecy concerning the coming of the Lord Jesus, about 700 years before, and so it came to pass exactly as he had said. (Micah 5:2).

The Old and New Testaments are interwoven with many such references to His birth, His suffering and death, His resurrection and Second Advent. All that was foretold has been accurately fulfilled; some prophecies in reference to His second coming yet await fulfilment. That too will come to pass according to the Scriptures.

Isaiah chapter 53 is a prime example of a prophecy which describes, even in detail, what is to befall the Lord Jesus. That prophet tells us, 'He is despised and rejected of men.' That was true while He was here on earth and it is still true today. Verse 8 says, 'He was taken from prison and from judgment: and who shall declare His generation.' He stood alone in Pilate's judgment hall; there was none to speak on His behalf, and none to plead His cause.

The Ethiopian eunuch, on his homeward journey in Acts chapter 8, was reading from Isaiah 53, verse 7, 'He is led as a Lamb to the slaughter,' Philip the evangelist had joined him in the chariot and the Ethiopian asked, "of whom speaketh the prophet this, of himself or of some other man?" And beginning at the same Scripture, Philip preached unto him Jesus.'

Verse 12 of Isaiah 53 tells us, 'He was numbered with the transgressors.' He was crucified between two thieves. In verse 9, 'He was with the rich in His death.' Joseph of Arimathea, a rich man, laid the body of our Lord in his own new tomb. 'He was afflicted, yet He opened not His mouth.' As He stood before Pilate He kept silent, so much so that Pilate marvelled.

The Psalmist David adds to this remarkable unfolding. Writing prophetically of the Lord Jesus in Psalm 22, in the very first verse he gives us one of the cries our Lord uttered on the cross: 'My God, my God, why hast thou forsaken Me?' In verse 16 he tells of the manner of His death. 'They pierced My hands and My feet.' The Jewish form of capital punishment was stoning, but here David speaks of crucifixion. How was David to know that Christ would be crucified or that the Romans would be involved in any way in Israel's history? Verse 13 records, 'They gaped upon Me with their mouths.' We think of the taunts of the mob around the cross. In verse 18 we read of the soldiers parting His garments among them; this they did, unwittingly fulfilling prophecy. (John 19:23).

The prophet Malachi foretold the coming of John the Baptist about 400 years before he came as a 'voice crying in the wilderness'. (Malachi 3:1). The Lord Jesus, speaking of him in Matthew 11:10, says, 'For this is he of whom *it is written*, "Behold I send My messenger before Thy face, which shall prepare Thy way before Thee".'

There are thirty-nine books in the Old Testament and twenty-seven in the New. These cover hundreds of years and are written by authors ranging in status from kings to fishermen. They comprise a marvellous collection of writings. I have touched a little on the remarkable way in which they are linked together; there is so much more!

Is there not a Divine Hand in all this? The men who were inspired to write these things lived centuries apart, so that in no way could they have contrived to bring those things together into one volume.

This is a wonderful Book, the life-giving Word of God! 'Blessed is he that readeth,' (Revelation 1:3). We who believe it, and endeavour to live by its principles, have not been deluded, nor have we 'followed cunningly devised fables', (2 Peter 1:16).

In it we have instructive history from the past, guidance for present day living, and 'we have the word of prophecy made more sure; whereunto we do well to take heed' (2 Peter 1:19).

A wise seaman would not set out on a voyage without a necessary chart. This is what the Bible is. Prudent men and women who follow its precepts and principles are on a right course, enjoying a wonderful journey, and with a glorious haven in prospect.

MAN THE MASTERPIECE

Man is the masterpiece of all that God created and made. Created on the sixth day, from the dust of the earth, he constitutes the final climax of all the work of creation. Made in the image of God, he is endowed with the physical senses of sight, hearing, taste, smell and touch. Yet over and above these natural powers, he possesses something which makes him different from the animal. The psalmist could say, 'I am fearfully and wonderfully made.' Man is said to have a 'conscience', that built-in sense that monitors his behaviour and betimes controls his activities. Animals generally move by instinct, unless they have been domesticated and trained. They have no code of morals, nor have they any knowledge of God.

There are divers views as to what is meant by man being made 'in the image of God.' In Genesis 3:22 we read, 'Behold the man is become as one of Us, to know good and evil.' Man is the only creature with an inherent knowledge of God; we can train and teach animals to do almost anything, but any attempt to teach them about God brings no reaction and no response.

When the early pioneer missionaries went out to the darkest

corners of heathendom they found men and women *who had never heard of God* worshipping idols of wood and stone and practising all sorts of spirit-motivated ideas and taboos. Here we have sure proof that man is on a higher plane than the animal and has knowledge of an unseen Supreme Power.

Man is capable of communication with God and God communicates with men; a communion initiated in the Garden of Eden. Beasts know nothing of this. The only 'worship' they know is fawning on and following their masters when trained and reared as pets.

We, on the other hand, have 'the knowledge of good and evil'. Our conscience reacts accordingly, so that we read of a good conscience, a pure conscience, and a seared conscience. We also have a limited knowledge of the future; some animals prepare for the future, but more by instinct than by intelligence. We know we will die, so we take precautions and avoid, as far as possible, situations of risk or danger. The lemmings of Norway, following some migratory urge, swim unwittingly to their death. Similarly the salmon stubbornly battles against the currents of its native river in order to gain the upper reaches, there to spawn and die.

No process of evolution or natural selection ever put man on this higher scale; this is a work of God. Man is the masterpiece that displays the workmanship of an all-wise Creator God.

PERSONAL EXPERIENCE

It has been said that what we are taught in childhood invariably makes us what we are as adults. There is no doubt that this is true, although with some exceptions. Those reared in Christian homes generally live by Christian principles; the Moslem child usually follows the teaching of his forebears. The sects of Christendom secure most of their followers from their children.

The writer was reared under the influence of the teaching of the Church of Scotland. Church attendance was compulsory, twice at the services on Sunday, and Sunday school was a 'must' for the younger members of the family.

As I grew older I felt there was something lacking in the preaching at the 'Kirk'. I continued in faithful attendance there until one day a company from the Salvation Army came from a neighbouring town to preach the gospel in our area. As I listened to the gospel message at that 'Army' open-air service, I realised that this was what I had been seeking but had failed to find at the Kirk. I made my way into the 'ring', and while kneeling in the roadway with the Officer I immediately knew and felt the power of saving grace. I knew that something had happened; I felt a power never experienced before. I cannot explain what transpired then, nor have I ever met a person with a like experience who can. But I do know now that this is what our Lord described as 'new birth.'

The Lord Jesus, speaking to Nicodemus in John chapter 3 of being 'born again', put it thus: 'The wind bloweth where it listeth, and thou hearest the sound thereof, but cannot tell whence it cometh, and whither it goeth, so is every one that is born of the Spirit.'

We cannot see the wind, but we can prove it is there; we feel it in our face and see the autumn leaves blown in the breeze. So is the unseen power of the Holy Spirit in one who is born again. The Apostle Paul, writing on the same theme, says: 'Therefore if any man be in Christ he is a new creature: old things are passed away; behold all things are become new.' (1 Cor.5:17).

I count myself a very ordinary member of the community. I spent most of my working life as a deep-sea fisherman – a special company (Psalm 107:23), and now, at 90 years of age, and after 70 years, I can testify that this 'new birth' is something real and genuine. None can refute this experience.

Millions of men and women have proved the power of God as I have done. It is said of the Lord Jesus, 'Wherefore He is able also to save them to the uttermost that come unto God by Him.' (Hebrews 7:25). None are outside the scope and power of sovereign grace. We may recall Mary Magdalene, out of whom were cast seven demons (Luke 8:2) as well as the unnamed woman at Sychar's well who had been living a life of sin and who had come to draw water from the well. There she met the Lord Jesus, who showed her the error of her ways and told her of 'living water' which He could give to all who believed in Him. All who taste of this 'living water' lose the desire for the 'broken cisterns', (Jeremiah 2:13) and the fleeting worldly pleasures this present day has to offer.

There are many 'trophies of grace' in our land; men and women who have lived lives of sin and dissipation, who have experienced this change in life, and can testify to the power of God in saving grace.

This is no illusion, nor have those who have undergone such a transformation been deluded. 'Whosoever believeth that Jesus is the Christ is born of God' (1 John 5:1). That is the sure promise of the glorious gospel; 'Christ Jesus came into the world to save sinners' (1 Timothy 1:15).

Here are some verses; I do not know the name of the author, but I do know that he/she and I have much in common.

Does God Exist?

THE MAJESTY OF GOD, AND HIS GRACE

I tried to measure time! Unmeasured years
Go back, but no *beginning* can I trace!
Behold God's glory! Vanish all my fears!
God Who has no beginning saves in GRACE.

I tried to pierce the future - life for aye:
I measured ages - ages keep not pace;
With love God had, and hath, and will display:
God without ending saves in wondrous GRACE.

I tried to measure space - no barrier find,
No terminus, no goal to boundless space.
Our thoughts must falter, helpless seems the mind;
God over all saves souls in glorious GRACE.

I tried to measure depth and height, and see
The grace that reached to meet my helpless case:
But I can only say, 'Christ died for me',
And I adore, o'erwhelmed by matchless GRACE.

THE QUERIES

Disasters occur from time to time throughout the world. On these occasions men and women generally give of their best, physically and financially, to help those affected by any such event.

Famines, floods, earthquakes, wars and disease, are never absent from us. Very many today ask: 'If there is a God of love up there, why are such things permitted? Why does He not intervene to prevent them? Such a question would suggest that God is to blame for these occurrences.

We have already observed that when God completed His work of creation all was pronounced very good. When Adam and Eve were created they were placed in ideal conditions for life and work, with one restriction. They were not to eat of 'the tree of life in the midst of the garden.' Under temptation they disobeyed God's command, with the result that sin and death has passed on to all subsequent generations, with all the tears and suffering which this has brought. The effects of their disobedience have touched the whole of creation, so that thistles, thorns, drought and floods are a part of our lives; and the beasts, over which the man had domination, have become wild

27

and aggressive, 'nature red in tooth and claw.'

The famines, so rife in Africa today, are caused mainly by 'man's inhumanity to man'. The civil wars and tribal conflicts there have reached inhuman proportions, so that the plight of the refugees has become a matter of international concern. It is a sad fact of this situation that all the time there is sufficient food on the earth to supply the needs of all. Throughout the E.E.C. the quantities of food in store are causing confusion and embarrassment to those in authority, and much is going to waste. The question of distribution to those in need is ever beset by problems political, financial, and military, and so thousands are dying daily in appalling conditions of hunger and disease. We can perceive a cruel irony in the fact that soldiers, in the same famine-stricken areas, all seem so healthy and well nourished while there is never any shortage of weapons and ammunition.

We who live under more favoured conditions have reason to be grateful for the blessings we enjoy, and more or less take for granted. We do know, however, that we are not immune from sickness and disease. This is the lot of all and has come to us as a result of Adam's disobedience.

While most of us require medical attention in some form throughout the normal pattern of life, we can bring evil upon ourselves by our behaviour and manner of life. We have only to think of the effects of smoking, the excessive use of alcohol, over-eating, or inordinate sexual activities.

The Bible shows very clearly the consequences of such behaviour and what the outcome will be of the flagrant immorality that is so wide-spread in our land today. (See Romans 1:25-32). There is a principle in life that touches us all. 'For whatsoever a man soweth, that shall he also reap. For he that soweth to his flesh shall of the flesh reap corruption; but he that soweth to the Spirit, shall of the Spirit reap life everlasting.' (Galations 6:7-8). None of us lives in insolation; our manner of life can, and often does, affect others.

Generally speaking among our contemporaries, divine precepts and principles are looked upon as out-of-date and lightly esteemed. Marriage has become an unnecessary bond, and equality of the sexes is regarded as progress and liberty. Yet God ordained partnership, not equality.

Sunday, the first day of the week, is a day for leisure and pleasure. Attendances for worship has in most instances declined, while church membership is usually a matter of convenience for such occasions as marriage, christenings and burial.

The accumulation of wealth and material things is considered to be success, while moral standards fall ever further into corruption and violence increases.

Any code of discipline, whether at school or elsewhere, is said to be an encroachment on civil and personal liberty.

The Lord Jesus left us an example that we should follow His steps. We can never hope to attain to the standards which He set, but if we endeavour in sincerity to obey His word, this world will be a safer and happier place.

Governments, of every political persuasion, have failed to stem the flood of crime and violence, caused mainly through the abuse of drugs and alcohol. Very many elderly folk live behind locked doors in fear of vandals, while women are afraid to walk our streets alone.

And as we come to recognise that the troubles and disasters so evident in the world are the result of sin, and of man's rejection of God and His word, God has decreed that all that Adam lost will yet be restored. The Lord Jesus is coming back to earth to reign in righteousness (Matthew 25:13).

'The wolf and the lamb shall feed together, and the lion shall eat straw like a bullock; and dust shall be the serpent's meat.' (Isaiah 65:25).

'Nation shall not lift up sword against nation, neither shall they learn war any more.' (Isaiah 2:4).

THE WORK OF GRACE
Tune - Speranza, 10.10.10.10.

O Lord our God; Jehovah Three in One,
Who spake the word of light, and it was done;
Creation's day displayed Thy mighty power,
Thy wisdom in that dark, primeval hour.

When we behold the worlds Thy Hands have made,
The heavens in star-filled glory there arrayed;
What then is man! that he should ever be
The object of redemption planned by Thee?

This work of grace, O Lord, doth far excel
Creation's glory, and to us does tell;
'Twas in Thy heart, ere worlds by Thee were formed,
That we to Jesus' image be conformed.

Amazing grace! And love no thought may scan,
Mercy and truth, united in the plan;
And in a Saviour, Jesus crucified,
Justice's demands are fully satisfied.

We ponder o'er what grace for us has done,
And see our sins all laid on Him, Thy Son;
That we through Him, to glory might be brought,
Arrayed in righteousness which He has wrought.

James Slater.

James Slater
1 Burnside Court
Portsoy
BANFF AB45 2QZ
Tel. 01261-843144